Spiritual Authority

An Apostolic Handbook On Religious Spirits

Apostle Dedric Hubbard

Published by Prophetic Fire Publishing

Tallahassee, Florida 32303

www.propheticfirepublishing.com

Table of Contents

Chapter 1.............................Order of Authority

Chapter 2..._Ephesus_............. Spirit of Religion

Chapter 3..._Smyrna_......Spirit of Intimidation
LOVELESS

Chapter 4._Pergamos_.....Spirit of Compromise

Chapter 5..._Thyatira_............Spirit of Control

Chapter 6...._Sardis_............Spirit of Tradition

Chapter 7._Philadelphia_....Spirit of Inferiority

Chapter 8..._Laodiceans_.............Spirit of Pride

Chapter 1

The Order of Authority

And having spoiled principalities and powers, he made a shew of them openly, triumphing over them in it.

Colossians 2:15

The church is in a state of ignorance when it comes to the knowledge and understanding of demons. And how they operate inside the boundaries of religion it's with this book based on knowledge shown to me by the Holy Spirit and my own spiritual encounters. I try to give an insight of the behavior and power assigned to the foundation of religion.

In this first chapter, The Order of Authority I will use it to show the legions of demons that are in religion. In this brief revelation, we will only highlight the key principalities of fallen angels. To understand the structure of demonic activity that is at work on Earth. The four main fallen angels that cause havoc on Earth are as described in the following:

Formalhut - and he is responsible for releasing demonic activity over the northern region of the earth. His name is defined as mouth of the whale.

Regulus – is the principle demon responsible for the demonic activity for the southern region of the world.

Aldebaran – is the principle demon responsible for demonic activity over the eastern region of the world.

Antares – is the principle demon responsible for the demonic activity over the western region of the world.

Now with these 4 major fallen angels controlling certain regions they have what I would call governors. That operate under them that help dispel the evil on the earth their names and functions in religious gatherings are as follows:

Azazel- is the principal fallen angel over non-denominational religion his name means God-strengthens this fallen angel enter the vessels when the watchers and/or fallen angels who are assigned to watch a move of God notices that God gives a person a vision and/or a place to be the spiritual authority in ministry. Without the counsel of a prophetic vessel for confirmation the vessel proceeds to develop a ministry under which they say God instructs them.

To develop a ministry, the person must understand basic biblical principles but, yet they fail to institute the foundation of God in their ministry plans Eph. 2:20. Which lays the foundation turns the ministry upon birth into a breeding ground for demonic activities all because it was started on the wrong foundation of Azazel who has them thinking they are moving in the strength of God.

Ananiel -is the guardian for Azazel for he is a watcher in which he looks for and notices the pattern of prophetic people only because they understand the damage a true prophet of God has encountered. This fallen angel is the one responsible for the foundation of God not being in the church for he seeks to enter the prophetic vessel to bring them under control to Azazel in which people think the pastors are the spiritual authority in God's church.

It is through Ananiel that Azazel knows when a prophet is being birth by God and thus when they can't access their spirit they use the vessels to begin condemning the prophet in which the prophet leaves so the fallen angel can still operate undetected by other prophetic vessels under their control.

Arakiel - is the evangelism angel for non-denominational ministries this fallen angel uses the spirit of agreement, familiarity, and inferiority to prey on those ignorant of God's true foundation. He promotes the church as one of a kind and is usually quite bold in speech and manner to those who are unexpected of God's true evangelism nature which is power evangelism. This fallen angel uses stealth, deception, and the fear of the Lord in their deceptive speech.

Marchosias - is the fallen angel that controls the knowledge of false prophetic vessel this fallen angel operates in intimidation, fear, manipulation, and witchcraft this vessel that is controlled by this fallen angel has pin-point accuracy in prophecies and revelations. You can only tell this angel by their order of authority in which they will point people to a man instead of the foundation of God.

When confronted or expose they will always retaliate in secret for they are abusers of authority this is the demon that has 98% of prophetic vessel in religious bondage for it's a religious prophetic vessel that it enters.

Naamah - This is the worship demon for the non-denominational religion it's no more than a singing whore selling her gift to the highest bidder this is also the demon that many prophetic people/speakers are in bondage too in which they charge you to hear the word or song of God. Their motives are money this demon fights for attention and will best be shown in a person of authority in which they must lead all the songs, loudest in the choir etc. This is also the demon that pairs with the homosexual spirit which is why most gays like to be the in thing in worship.

Now it is of interest to note the order of the fallen angels are correct, but their position of authority is what I found amazing for we understand God works in straight order according to those who have the most spiritual authority in God's foundation.

Although Azazel is the leader it is of interest that Marchosias is in charge for it must be among the people to communicate with Annaniel. In which pastors who have prophetic anointing or who operate in a spirit of fear receives their messages from Marchosias and thus the sheep thinks it's a word from the lord.

Because Marchosias is an abuser of authority he uses different vessels to speak bold of your spiritual leaders. To keep fear of the weak vessel the fallen angel Azazel has taken control of what they feed the sheep. This is done to instill inferiority of the sheep Azazel feeds from spiritually. Once the vessel has been strengthened with enough dead spirits the other angels enter the leader with stolen dreams, ideas, and knowledge.

When the leader (Azazel) wants to know how much power he has he brings an idea before the church and the vessel that has this knowledge comes forth in agreement it will usually be the one in authority. And thus, your non-denominational religion gives all their power to a leader.

So, when they pray because of the covenant with these fallen angels they think they are talking to God but it's Azazel which answers their prayer. Thus, when they go outside of their covenant and come to a prophet such as me it goes against anything they have been taught and/or heard because we listen to the God of a man and not a man that many have made a God. It's imperative that now as many who have purchase and read this book understand the power and authority of the fallen angels.

As a leader you must put all pride aside and ask yourself am, I being controlled by a fallen angel? Self – examination is critical when new revelation is released as it teaches to see are, we still teachable. Most leaders say they are teachable but when challenge to change their ways when trust is released, they rather hold to their religious ways of ministry.

So, as we close this chapter the reason why these fallen angels continue in power is because of the 7 spirits that are listed in the book of Revelation. As I have examined the 7 churches, they all had 1 key spirit that allowed the works of satan to enter which is the cause of why most people are in bondage to religion.

Chapter 2

The Spirit of Religion

Nevertheless, I have somewhat against thee, because thou hast left thy first love.

Revelation 2:4

As we begin to deal with the first sprit that oftentimes leads the church astray, we must understand that each church in the book of revelation. Had an angel that was assigned to govern or direct the path of the church. Some say it's the pastor of the church while some say it was an actual angel. But for the sake of revelation whatever you believe is your opinion. What matter most is how does your ministry runs? The spirit of religion runs rampantly inside many churches today and mainly because of leadership.

Today's leadership has turned away from the Holy Spirit and revelation of the word to instill their own human interpretation. In doing this they preach, speak, and teach more about money and carnal materialistic matters.

More than holiness, deliverance and the power that lies in one's soul. It's of interest for me to point out that Ephesus name means desirable. It was located on the Aegean Sea, had a beautiful harbor, and was situated on the main highway for the region.

It also held one of the Seven Wonders of the World, the temple to Diana (Artemis), pagan goddess of fertility. So, why is that important to mention? It's because and this is just my opinion that we understand that satan likes deception and counterfeiting the things of God. So, I would say that the believers of Ephesus stop producing spiritually. Because of the influence that the temple of Diana may have caused.

Pastor Ron Phillips described it like this: The church at Ephesus had "left their first love". As we study the book of revelation and examine the church at Ephesus, we can see they were doctrinally sound and had everything in order.

But they had lost their passion and zeal for the things of God. When you turn to Acts 19 to look at the first works and first love you discover an astounding truth.

At the birth of the Ephesian church they were baptizing in water, laying hands on the people for the baptism of the Holy Spirit, magnifying God in tongues, casting out demons, healing with prayer cloths, and being evicted from the old order.

The church at Ephesus had every element of church life in order and they were a hard-working congregation. Yet the fire, the passion, the love had gone out of it. We see now that religion had taken over with its dull duty and tired traditionalism. The power of God was missing; demons were no longer leaving, tongues were absent, miracles were simply a memory. A loveless routine of religious works had replaced the power and passion of the Holy Spirit.

So, now as we can see even with this current dispensation of church the routine of religion has crept into the daily growth of the church.

The key to understanding is in Revelation 2:2 which states: I know thy works, and thy labour, and thy patience, and how thou canst not bear them which are evil: and thou hast tried them which say they are apostles, and are not, and hast found them liars:

The leading authority of the church had become worthless the apostolic order was now in the hands of liars. It saddens me how believers can see their leaders not operating in the things of God. But, refuse to confront them about their behavior. Thereby, allowing many to be deceived with false teachings and unrealistic expectations.

As I write this book, I believe we can see the evidence of the prophetic revelation that John released generations ago. If we take inventory of certain ministries operations, we can see many are not following the word of God. As, I write this book for example many tongue talking believers will celebrate Halloween. ** Those that say they don't celebrate Halloween will do trunk or treat and the world celebrates it as a fall festival.

Now 2nd Timothy 1:7 states For God hath not given us the spirit of fear; but of power, and of love, and of a sound mind. So, do we as believers during this season look for ways to instill fear? It's this twisted mindset of believers that we must snap out of if we want to operate in the true power and authority of God.

And yet, we may never see that power because the spirit of religion has the church bound unto the traditions of men. Forgoing the written word of God to follow man-made bondages and doctrine that is rooted and grounded in hierarchy and not the spirit of God.

When the church programs are based on knowing when to play worship music, when to pray, when to teach then its no room for the Holy Spirit to have free course because if it doesn't follow the established written routine it's considered not of God. But as we bring this chapter to a close as leaders look over how you say you worship God is it programmed or does the Holy Spirit have free reign?

Chapter 3

Spirit of Intimidation

And unto the angel of the church in Smyrna write; These things saith the first and the last, which was dead, and is alive;

In this chapter we will deal with the spirit of intimidation. This spirit I believe has run rampant within the last 13-20 years in the gospel of Christ. In Revelation 2:9 it states I know thy works, and tribulation, and poverty, (but thou art rich) and *I know* the blasphemy of them which say they are Jews, and are not, but *are* the synagogue of Satan. I feel this to be a prophetic model of the structure of some of today's leaders in ministry. As they use the gifts of God as a hierarchy of power to spread fear among the believers in their ministries.

Thus, using fear of questioning anything leadership does equates questioning God. So, the people sit quietly taking the abuse and ungodlike demands put on them as servitude to their leaders. But what is the cause when encountering leaders who use intimidation to control the sheep?

Low self-esteem is the cause for intimidating leaders as believers if you can listen in when they give testimonies of their childhood you will see the traits of low self-esteem.

In fact, while researching for this book Thomas Rainer listed 14 key traits that intimidating leaders used, and they are listed as follows:

They rarely demonstrate the fruit of the Spirit. Paul notes those specific attributes in Galatians 5:22-23: love, joy, peace, patience, kindness, goodness, faith, gentleness, and self-control. You won't see them much in toxic leaders.

They seek a minimalist structure of accountability. Indeed, if they could get away with it, they would operate in a totally autocratic fashion, with heavy, top down leadership.

They expect behavior of others they don't expect of themselves. "Do as I say, not as I do."

They see almost everyone else as inferior to themselves. You will hear them criticizing other leaders while building themselves up.

They show favoritism. They have a favored few while they marginalize the rest.

They have frequent anger outbursts. This behavior takes place when they don't get their way.

They say one thing to some people, but different things to others. This is a soft way of saying they lie.

They seek to dismiss or marginalize people before they attempt to develop them. People are means to their ends; they see them as projects, not God's people who need mentoring and developing.

They are manipulative. Their most common tactic is using partial truths to get their way.

They lack transparency. Autocratic leaders are rarely transparent. If they get caught abusing their power, they may have to forfeit it.

They do not allow for pushback or disagreement. When someone does disagree, he or she becomes the victim of the leader's anger and marginalization.

They surround themselves with sycophants. Their inner circle thus often includes close friends and family members, as well as a host of "yes people."

They communicate poorly. Any clarity of communication would reveal their autocratic behavior, so they keep their communications unintelligible and obtuse.

They are self-absorbed. In fact, they would unlikely see themselves in any of these symptoms.

Do these 14 traits fit in your current church structure? If so, it's my opinion that your run fast to a place of peace and solitude. So, as we close this chapter look over these 14 traits as a leader and a believer. If they are operating in your ministry as a leader it would be wise to begin to make changes as a believer I would go to God and ask him to show you what you need to do.

Chapter 4

Spirit of Compromise

And to the angel of the church in Pergamos write; These things saith he which hath the sharp sword with two edges;

COMPROMISE:

 - To make liable to danger
 - To reduce the quality, value or degree of something

The definition of compromise is very valuable to understand for this chapter of this book. Mainly, because when you begin to compromise for a person, place or thing. Then you not only weaken the foundation on which you are building but you put in danger anything that surrounds what you have built.

Compromising runs rampant now in the church many are preaching their thoughts, perceptions and opinions the bible is not the source of reference anymore. It's no secret that the city of Pergamos name is defined as height; elevation.

Which means pride is the cause of compromising it saddens my heart as a believer. When we as followers of Christ partake in worldly and pagan activities especially in these paganistic holidays.

We reduce the feasts God has instructed us to partake of that is listed in the Bible to hold on to the pagan traditions of heathens. Many leaders in today's ministries fail to hold their followers as well as people in leadership position accountable to their actions. Having people unaccountable to their choice leaves room for them to compromise in other areas of their lives.

One thing the leaders I mentor and the sheep I am responsible for always mention to me. Is that they like how I can see their wrong choices, decisions and actions in the spirit. Then come to them in such a way that it makes them want to live right. If the true bride of Christ is going to come forth the leaders in today's dispensation. Then the leaders must begin to revamp, reteach and reassess their ways of ministering.

We see in scripture the church at Pergamos suffered a similar fate that is happening in today's church. Let's examine the scripture and it reads as follows:

But I have a few things against thee, because thou hast there them that hold the doctrine of Balaam, who taught Balac to cast a stumbling block before the children of Israel, to eat things sacrificed unto idols, and to commit fornication. We have many leaders and prophets that are operating according to the spirit of Balaam. They are not speaking the word of God but compromising the word for money, notoriety and publicity.

As 2020 approaches if you are a leader and happen to read this book, I implore you to find a true gift to come and reevaluate your ministry. Even as I write I have been contacted by a few leaders in different parts of the country. That are inquiring about me coming and giving them apostolic guidance and oversight of their ministry. Because they have seen no growth or feel their ministries are in a slump.

As bishops over the souls of people in your congregation 2020 is a year you need to have a complete evaluation of your ministry. In order to make sure you are not operating in a ministry of compromise.

Chapter 5

Spirit of Control

And unto the angel of the church in Thyatira write; These things saith the Son of God, who hath his eyes like unto a flame of fire, and his feet *are* like fine brass;

In this chapter we deal with one of the most dangerous spirit that resides in about 98% of today's churches. The spirit of control is dangerous and is very easy to pinpoint but is often overlooked. Because of the structure in today's religious churches as we use 1st 12:28 as the foundational scripture for this revelation.

It reads as follows: And God hath set some in the church, first apostles, secondarily prophets, thirdly teachers, after that miracles, then gifts of healings, helps, governments, diversities of tongues. As many wonder why would I choose this scripture which shows an order but leaves out the pastor and evangelist gifting.

It's because we are entering in a dispensation in which those two gifts will begin to fade away. As it relates to positional authority in your local churches. Its because when the church use the gifts in order as taught by Christ.

When the gifts are not operating or accepted in the body of Christ as it relates to what is in the Bible. It allows witchcraft to take root through the spirit of control.

An article written by Derek Prince teaches on 4 levels of witchcraft they are as follows:

1. **Open/Public Witchcraft** - Operating in its real nature, witchcraft teaches and practices the worship of Satan. The Church of Satan has its own web site on the Internet, which presents it as a "respectable" church.

But those who have come out of its clutches will tell you that the central satanic ceremony is a "black mass"–a blasphemous parody of a Christian Communion service.

The dominant motivation is a deliberate, conscious hatred and rejection of Jesus Christ. It is vital to note that the main enemy of witchcraft is not Islam, humanism or some Eastern religion; it is the Christian Church.

2. **Underground Witchcraft** - covens usually meet at night to offer sacrifices and to initiate new members. One central element in the practice of witchcraft is sacrifice. Usually the sacrifices are small animals (dogs, cats, rats, etc.). Sometimes, though, a sacrifice is human. Without doubt, the god of witchcraft is Satan. Its adherents are bound to him and to one another by a covenant committing them to absolute secrecy concerning their activities.

3. **Fifth Column/Disguised** - There are many forms of philosophy and religion that are rooted in witchcraft. The fifth column operation of witchcraft– the forms operating within the guise of accepted practice–is continually expanding.

New Age studies, hypnosis and acupuncture are but a few of the many forms taken by witchcraft to entice innocent people into the territory of Satan.

4. **A Work of the Flesh** - Now that we have examined three main forms of witchcraft as a supernatural force–the public form, the underground form, and the fifth column–we must expose the root. It is the least recognized operation, but it permeates society and the Church. In Galatians 5:19–21 Paul lists the works of the "flesh" ("sinful nature," NIV).

In the middle he mentions "idolatry, sorcery" (NKJV) or "idolatry and witchcraft" (NIV). This nature often manifests itself, even in infancy, in efforts to control other people. We feel secure if we can control others. Conversely, God never seeks to control us. He respects the free will He has given each of us, although He does hold us responsible for how we use that freedom.

There are three ways they desire to control expresses itself: manipulation, intimidation and domination. The goal is domination. People who recognize that they are weaker than those they seek to control tend to manipulate; those who feel stronger tend to intimidate.

But the end purpose is the same: to dominate–that is, to control others and get them to do what we want. Many family relationships portray these expressions.

Why was important to list these four major levels of witchcraft? I am glad you asked it's because that is what today's churches are operating through. It is a mixture of levels 3 and 4 remember earlier when I said the spirit of control is hard to detect. It's because it has become standard practice to have pastors have total control of the church. Without apostolic or prophetic oversight yet have them in the church. Therefore, the church is out of order instead of pastors reporting or submitting to the apostles.

The apostle and prophets submitting to the pastors and most often the pastors do not understand the anointing of these 2 powerful gifts sent from God. For the true anointing of God and the power of the Holy Spirit to flow in the church. Many pastors must submit to the established leadership accountability that is listed in the Bible.

Chapter 6

Spirit of Tradition

And unto the angel of the church in Sardis write; These things saith he that hath the seven Spirits of God, and the seven stars; I know thy works, that thou hast a name that thou livest, and art dead.

We now deal with another major spirit that will kill the birthing of a church. Which is the spirit of tradition although there are plenty of spiritual tradition throughout the church. I will only deal with the one that is relevant to the revelation of this book. What we must understand if we are to see a moving and living church endowed with power from God. Leaders cannot be blind to change many of today's leaders are the rule makers and breakers. They rarely listen to anything that will bring the church to the next level if the leader does not believe it's of God.

Now I am not saying that some people may not be speaking from the mouth of God. But just supposed if the gifts were placed properly in the church especially the prophetic gifting. Because after all scripture says God will not do anything without first revealing it to his prophets. Which is why so many churches are behind in the revelation and movements of God.

It's because if the leader of a church does not have a prophetic anointing nor anyone who has a relationship with God.

It means leaders are not getting the fresh revelations and downloaded which are needed to move the church and the believers forward. Herein is the battle that we who are called to turn the church back to God under the operation of the Holy Spirit. Meet most of our problems very few leaders if any wants to change their way of ministry.

Most leaders I have found in traveling the country preaching the gospel. Are intimidated by people in their ministries. I have seen with my own eyes that sometimes the people in the pews are more anointed then the leaders that teach them. With that we see many of today's churches represent the church of Sardis they show full of life and riches.

But only because the people come in the buildings dressed in their fancy clothes, luxury cars talking about all the materialistic things God has blessed them with. Only to leave out empty spiritually rarely do you hear any talking of experiencing supernatural signs, wonders and miracles. And to be honest most of them struggling to keep the materialistic things they brag about while in church.

A church that is spiritually dead cannot breathe life into the souls that migrate through there doors. It is non effective we live in a day and time where most ministries brag and gloat about having 1 church in 3 locations. But the leader has no spiritual connection with the people in those locations. One thing I drive home to leaders I have mentored or leadership conferences I have attended. Is that if you have no word from God for any person in your congregation that person is not assigned to your ministry.

When people come visit my ministry and I have not received a word from God. Concerning who they are, their calling, and how do I minister to them within a month. I meet with them personally and tell them they can stay and listen if they desire. But in a leadership capacity I cannot effectively minister to their needs because God has not revealed their destiny to me.

I do this so a person will not become what I call pew dead in which they sit in the congregation enjoying the services. But not experiencing any spiritual growth, revelations or instructions from God.

What this approach does is keep a ministry alive, thriving and moving in the spirit of God. Because everyone knows who they are, the calling they have, and as a result they move in different ways according to the leading of the Holy Spirit.

But this takes a confident leader to be able to allow a church to operate truly by God's spirit. I'm not jealous of anyone's calling or gifting which allows me more freedom to use different people at different times. For the church to come out of it's zombie like state there must be leaders who are willing to restructure their ministries.

And allow new leadership oversight to come in and tell them spiritually what the weakness and strength are they see in the ministry. Then allow them to make changes as such or many ministries will miss a mandated move of God.

Chapter 7

Spirit of Inferiority

And to the angel of the church in Philadelphia write; These things saith he that is holy, he that is true, he that hath the key of David, he that openeth, and no man shutteth; and shutteth, and no man openeth;"

The spirit of inferiority has damaged more people as well as hampered the growth of ministries. In ways that many cannot even comprehend or begin to think about one reason for this is not understand their calling. According to Herman Hoeksema in an article he wrote the following observation: One of the chief characteristics of the church in Philadelphia is undoubtedly expressed in the words of the Savior, "Thou hast a little strength." This describes her outward condition in the world.

 The meaning is that the church was small. This was one of her most emphatic traits. We understand, of course, that this does not imply that the other churches were outwardly great and strong: for this was not the case.

 In fact, we may undoubtedly say that the church in general, the true church of Jesus Christ, is always of little power if compared with the strength of the world. It is always comparatively small in numbers. It usually is financially poor. It does not count among its numbers the rich and the great of the world.

And therefore, it is evident that in a general sense what the Savior here writes about the church in Philadelphia may be said of all the churches addressed thus far. Ephesus, Smyrna, Pergamos, Thyatira, and Sardis, -all were small and poor and of little strength according to the measure of the world. Nevertheless, of the church in Philadelphia this was especially and emphatically true.

It was not the chief characteristic of the other churches, but it was one of the main features of the church in Philadelphia. We may take it, therefore, that in this little sentence the Lord gives a brief description of the peculiar situation in the church of Philadelphia from an external point of view.

However, when the Lord addresses the church in Philadelphia thus, and remarks that she has but little strength, this refers only to her outward position in the world. It does not describe her spiritual condition. Spiritually the little church in Philadelphia was not weak, but strong indeed. That this is true is evident from rest of the letter addressed to her.

The Lord commends her for having kept His Word, which implies that the church remained faithful to the truth of the gospel. And thus, to keep the Word of Jesus certainly requires spiritual strength. The church that is spiritually weak certainly will not keep the Word of Jesus.

Always the enemies encompass the church of Jesus Christ in the world; and always those enemies attack her especially from the viewpoint of the truth. It requires strength, spiritual strength, the exercise of the power of faith, to be faithful to the truth and to keep the Word of the Lord.

This is emphasized in what follows immediately. It is evident that the church had not only kept the Word of Jesus, but also confessed His name. For the Lord writes to her: "Thou hast not denied my name." The negative form of this expression implies that the enemies, perhaps especially the Jews of Philadelphia, had exerted all their influence to make the church deny the name of Christ.

They persecuted her and left her but little standing room in the midst of the world. But this negative expression also implies, by way of contrast, that the church in Philadelphia had openly confessed the name of the Lord Jesus Christ. They could not and did not keep still about that name of their glorious Lord and Redeemer, in Whom they believed and

Whom they loved, who had delivered them from sin and death and merited for them everlasting life and glory. Of course, all this points to real spiritual strength.

What needs to happen leaders with small ministries need to understand that size does not always matter. Even when I begin ministry back in 2006 it was just me. I had no following, no support, no financial backing but I did hear God's voice and that was good enough for me.

So, here I am this love wolf going against ministries with millions of dollars and followers.

But way when God seen I was prepared I begin to get more exposure in fact from 2011-2013 I had the #1 prophetic website in the world. I begin to gain dedicated followers who supported me financially as well as spiritually. Now I wasn't rich in ministry money, but I had enough coming in where I was now able to travel freely to preach the gospel.

Even now I get excited when people come to me and ask me to plant a church, help the begin or ministry or show them the power God has inside of them. I am saying this because to some who read this book you must understand never feel inferior to anyone. Your day is coming if you stay the course.

You must not be a leader who is intimidated at the growth and support that you may see other leaders are getting. This will cause you to compromise your true intent of the reason God has called you into ministry. In this 2020 season as leaders and believers in God you must not allow the spirit of inferiority to take root in anything that you do.

Chapter 8

Spirit of Pride

And unto the angel of the church of the Laodiceans write; These things saith the Amen, the faithful and true witness, the beginning of the creation of God;

Now as we begin to close out the book with this last chapter, I find it befitting the last chapter is on the spirit of pride. This spirt of pride is at an all time high in today's ministries. You can tell by the way they dress to impress on Sundays as they look for all the oohhs and aaas of fellow church members. Pride destroys a ministry before it even begins as leaders make up bylaws, salaries and how they wish to be approached.

Most people that operate in the spirit of pride stems from either low self-esteem or rejection. So, when they finally get the attention of the people, they want to feel important and feared at the same time. Let's just do a recap of how God sent messages to all several churches.

Five churches with serious problems have already been addressed, and they are on somewhat of a descending scale. As you move through the seven letters, remember two of them had no condemnation, that's Smyrna and Philadelphia, the other five progressively degenerate.

There was Ephesus, the church still strong doctrinally, but the church that left its first love. There was Pergamos, which had not denied the faith but was tolerating sin. There was Thyatira where there were still some good things going on but full-blown compromise with evil had taken place and the majority seemed to have been involved.

Then there was Sardis, a church with only a few genuine believers, a church which had a name but was actually dead. And now at the bottom, if you will, is Laodicea. This is an unsaved church. In fact, if there were any believers in this church, they aren't even referred to in the letter at all.

It is a church that is characterized by lukewarmness which becomes a metaphor for being non-saved people. Laodicea has the grim distinction of being, among all seven letters, the only one in which Christ has nothing good to say.

It is unmitigated, unspared condemnation. There is in this church, apparently, absolutely no redeeming feature. This is the unsaved, unregenerate false church. Also, because of the nature of the church, this is the most threatening epistle. This is the most blistering rebuke. And it is sent to a proud church. Therein is the problem in this dispensation most of the ministries have become proud.

They are proud in their logos, pastors, doctrine, dress and their worship to God. But once again they are not having any life-changing supernatural manifestations among the people in their congregation. If we are once again dominate these other religions, we must go back to the basics.

And hear what the new apostolic/prophetic voices are saying. As well as being opened to be retaught, reread the Bible review revelations that has been taught. But does not line up with the word of God in fact we must go back to line upon line and precept among precept.

We are in a dangerous time in the body of Christ where we need to show the power of Christ strong to a world that is dying and being overtaken by sin. No longer can leaders be a partaker of the sin they so boldly preaching against. Thereby as I close this book out, I hope there was something said, or a revelation released to get you. To identify, destroy and refurbish your ministries to the proper protocol that God has left as a guideline for us in his Bible.